Confucius Said ...

A Management Book
For The 21st Century

W.J. "Duke" Mader

ISBN: 1-4637-9647-1
ISBN-13: 9781463796471

Dedication

The mantle of success comes in all sizes colors and fabrics: awards we have won, accomplishments we have achieved, milestones we have reached. I can say with great satisfaction that I have enjoyed a fulfilling life and have achieved the endorsement of three exceptional children: Yvonne, John II, and Christopher*. I couldn't be prouder of these three children. They have honored me with my own special pedestal. In all the world there is no greater joy a parent can know than the love and respect of his children. I dedicate this book to my children.

I spent 15 years writing and rewriting this manuscript. It was my beautiful wife, Zita, who finally convinced me to finish the book and take it to print. I love you, Z!

(*Christopher was murdered in 2004.)

CONTENTS

FORWARD

Did you ever have one of those days when you woke up on the wrong side of the bed, looked out the window and wished the whole world would trip? I recall a day like that many years ago, it was a very hectic day, one of those days when absolutely nothing went right. The previous day's paperwork was late going to the home office. The bank called to say the deposit was short, and I had one of those token employees who had the uncanny ability to not only never get anything accomplished himself, but also prevent others from getting their work done. He had been following me around all morning asking me the same meaningless question. You know the kind without any real answer. The kind of question that, if it did have an answer, would be arguable.

By trying to ignore this troublesome employee I had hoped that he would forget his mission in life and go on to other things. None the less, this persistent thorn kept throbbing until he drove me to a point where I had forgotten all the seminars I had ever attended on managing difficult employees. Books, tapes and magazine articles I had read and lectures I had attended all faded under the reality of frustration. Not having a meaningful answer to give this person was bad enough, but having to answer a non-question was worse.

Finally I turned and blurted out, "Does your nose itch?"

"No, sir."

"Good, then don't scratch it."

I have since learned to ask, "Why doesn't your nose itch?" just to keep from getting in a rut. It had the same results. I was able to confuse the confused. By turning the situation around I was able to escape my two-legged menace and send him away talking to himself. Later that same day during break I overheard him say to some of the other employees, "Do you know what Mr. Mader told me?"

I suppose in some strange way it parallels the old adage, "If it isn't broken, don't fix it."

There are all sorts of books on management written today, books for almost every occasion: upper level management, corporate management, managing the masses, managing a few employees, or managing a department. The manager of a small group of employees uses a different management system than his corporate counterpart who manages blocks of employees, rather than the hands on management style of the small businessman.

Group leaders manage specific groups usually doing pretty much the same things, or same types of duties. A small businessman must have total knowledge of his business and be able to motivate and provide leadership for all his employees. No matter what the job description or pay scale is, from dishwashers to head cooks, from stock clerks to purchasing agents, the small businessman must communicate to each employee on their own level.

World famous magician Houdini once said, "The best trick is an old one done exceptionally well, rather than a new one done poorly." Throughout the many years of management books and seminars, there have not been too many new concepts, but many old ones revisited time and time again. It is the purpose of this book to revisit some of the more important ideas and concepts that have stood the test of time. I hope you are familiar with "Ancient Oriental Proverbs"—proverbs, or sayings of wisdom from the old masters if you wish. Western culture has long been fascinated with them and Eastern culture still lives by them. I believe this is why the Japanese and other Oriental cultures exceed Western cultures when it comes to managing and motivating people.

Please read twice:

A long time ago a very successful teacher told her class that the reason she was so successful and the reason her students scored so high on their tests was due to her special secret.

"First I tell them what it is I am going to teach them, then I teach them, then I tell them what I taught them."

Her point being that most people do not get the full value of the information they are trying to obtain the first time. This was her way of drilling information into their heads.

I have been reading books on Oriental religions for a long time and have acquired a sizable library. Oriental philosophy has been quoted for thousands of years. The more I read the more similarities I found between the thinking and doing of thousands of years ago and today. Oriental wisdom was harvested in the same fertile fields that produce much of today's reasoning and doings. I was surprised to find so many of today's type of problems have solutions dating back many thousands of years.

Oriental management practices that parallel our own modern day situations are the most interesting and useful. I studied Oriental writings with references to the 'way' of management. The Oriental 'way', after being translated into today's terms and technologies, is remarkable. Fortunately many of the terms and situations translate almost literally. Of course, thousands of years ago there was no technology as we know it. However, the basics for understanding the human being and knowing how to motivate people into being the best they can be, is, and always has been, the same. While man has come out of the Stone Age and replaced caves with condominiums, the basic human being has not changed. Our phobias, talents, abilities, and wisdom may have grown up, but the building blocks that make up our character remain the same.

The following chapters are my interpretations of concepts from other writings. Once we get past the early concepts and progress into more modern times it becomes easier to read.

Oriental businessmen have a worldwide reputation for being shrewd leaders because of their determination to succeed. In the following pages you will find the same philosophy they learn like a Bible, before they are allowed to progress in their chosen field. It must be remembered that Oriental philosophy is very basic and to the point, just like their paintings. The beauty of the thought is found in its simplicity. Please bear with me as I refer to the 'way' of management as being the 'way' that the Orientals have been learning for centuries. As you read and experience this manuscript you may recognize concepts that you have studied and many of you may have practiced. I am sure you will be surprised to learn that many seemingly new ideas are thousands of years old.

chapter 1

WHILE MANY BOOKS on management have been written since the industrial revolution the one that has impressed me the most is an Oriental Classic, "A BOOK OF FIVE RINGS," written over three hundred years ago by one of Japan's most renowned warriors, Miyamotto Musashi. That's right, he was a famous warrior, not a businessman or a scholar, not a learned man of degrees, but a man of uncanny insight into human nature and a person dedicated to the 'way'. His book, dedicated to the art of strategy, is still used today as an achievement guide for the modern Japanese businessman and followed with the same zest and success today that motivated Musashi then, further demonstrating the old saying of "nothing new."

The strategy we are studying here is strategy as it relates to management. "What," you might ask, "does a barbarian know about the fine art of management?" There are very few managers in the world today who understand the 'way' of strategy as it relates to management, and none have written with such clarity as the ancient Orientals.

There are two basic, uniquely intertwined concepts or laws to the 'way' of strategy. The first is the 'way' of learning: mastering the scope of, and understanding the principles of how to manage successfully. The second law of the 'way' of strategy is: creating reality from concept, or reproducing reality to a more comfortable and useful practicality. Of what use is a brilliant idea if it cannot be written down, verbalized, or expressed. Knowledge without the ability to translate the same into meaningful action or coherent reality is useless.

Even if a person has no natural ability he can learn how to be a manager by sticking faithfully to both divisions of the 'way'. It can be said the 'way' of the manager is a resolute acceptance to dedication, or focus. Dedication is a virtue shared by many, it is not the sole property of management. The main difference being, the manager, while studying the 'way' of strategy, will gain many small victories by crossing ideas with individuals. With a few, or a large number of employees, he can attain power and recognition for both himself and his company. This is a virtue of strategy is a virtue of the 'way'.

I find there are very few men know the answer to the question, "What is the 'way' of the manager?" The 'way' of the manager is to be dedicated to an absolute. This means choosing dedication whenever there is a choice between success and failure. It means being willing to see things to finality, being resolved. "To die not having reached your goal, without having spent time in honest pursuit of it is to die uselessly." If you maintain your spirit from morning to night, accustomed to the idea of dedication and resolve, then consider yourself becoming one with the 'way' of the manager. Then it is said you can pass through life with no possibility of failure and able to perform the duties and the demands that your position requires.

The goal is to encourage the employee to think earnestly of the business of his employer, to take a position of ownership and pride in his work that will reflect in self fulfillment. This is the type of employee all management seeks to hire. I am not speaking of hiring an employee who is already trained and can begin work right away with little or no supervision. That is not a good hire. That is an excuse for management not to fulfill its obligation to the 'way'. Even an employee who seems completely useless is a trusted co-worker, if he does nothing more than to work honestly towards the welfare of his employer. While some employees are prone to sudden bursts of inspiration, there are others who do not come by good ideas easily but arrive at an answer only after slow and deliberate evaluation. If we look further into the matter we find even though people's natural abilities may differ, when your thinking rises above concern for your own welfare, then wisdom, which is altogether independent of thought, appears. Remember, no two people think exactly alike. Every problem will have as many answers as there are people submitting solutions. While many answers may seem similar in nature, their recipe for completion will differ as greatly as the persons submitting them. Do not think that just because you are the manager and are in charge, your answer or solution is necessarily the best. By choosing the avenue best for the company and by having the maturity to understand the path others would have you follow, the best solution will be had. This is the 'way' of choice. Take time and ponder this concept, understand it well. It is a building block of the 'way'.

There are people who think deeply on things, and, though they may carefully consider the future they will usually think around the basis of their own welfare. They make certain the solution they choose casts them in a primary role. It is very difficult for narrow-minded people to rise above thinking about their own welfare. Before you embark on a new challenge, put your self-ishness behind you and remember the four ancient oaths of the masters: Never be late with respect to the 'way' of the manager, be useful to your God, be respectful to your parents, go beyond love and grief, and exist for the good of mankind. In ancient China and Japan practitioners of the 'way' have been known as masters of strategy. Managers must learn this 'way'. There are many people in this world who think of themselves as managers but are only sitting in the bleachers of life, close enough to watch, but far enough away to keep from getting personally involved.

"This way," or "That way," or "Every which way," are all using the term 'way' to refer to something specific. A person waiting to go on a trip must know the "way." Former New York Yankee great, Yogi Berra, said "If you don't know where you're going you will probably end up somewhere else." The 'way' of the manager is strategy. His ability to master this strategy is a reflection on his success as a manager, and how he learns the strategy is his way of formulating and practicing success.

If we look at the world today we see abilities or talents for sale. Today it is commonplace for people to use electronic media to sell themselves: from reality shows to commercials to news media to politicians trying desperately to sell themselves to voters. In this closed world of strategy those teaching and those learning their concepts are more concerned with the coloring or staging of their ideas or techniques. These pretend students of the 'way' are merely looking for quick profits and benefits. This leads to immature strategy, which is usually followed by grief. Be wary of those who preach uncomplicated solutions to complex problems. When so much attention is given to the solution and not the result it is because the manager is too busy making himself look good. It is the immature manager who may briefly bask in a fading artificial light of success only to then face the real strength in the weakness of the solution.

There are, of course, others who know the 'way'. Managers are not the only people who possess a map and compass. There are four basic groups of people with success in mind who will follow their own 'way'. These groups are: The soldier, the merchant, the artists or craftsman and the farmers. Of course there are endless sub-groups, but according to the ancient masters these are the main groups.

The farmer must have knowledge of the seasons as well as agricultural equipment to complete his mission. The 'way' of the farmer is filled with pitfalls and disappointment. His rewards are almost completely controlled by forces outside his influence. Careful, well thought out plans can change with an ill-fated wind. He is at the mercy of the heavens and the appetite of mankind.

The carpenter uses a master plan to build a structure, and the 'way' of strategy here is very similar in that there is a need to have a campaign or blueprint for action. The carpenter must make many decisions: the type of woods to be used to the best benefit of the project, the type of stones and other such materials. He must know which laborers and technicians to delegate tasks to if he is to get the most for his employer. If the carpenter places his men properly the finished product will be good. The carpenter must take into account the abilities and limitations of his crew, observing them, asking nothing of them that is unreasonable. He must keep up their morale and encourage them whenever necessary. That is his principle of strategy. That is adherence to the 'way'. The achievement of the carpenter is that his work is not flawed, the joints not misaligned, the sections all fit well and the finished project is a reflection of a well-planned idea.

To learn the 'way' ponder these things written here one at a time and study them.

The merchant must obtain products and sell them for a living. The 'way' of the merchant is to live by taking a profit. To do this he must understand the difference between needs and wants, while catering to the fantasy and ego of his customer. For it is the appetite of the ego that can never be satisfied.

The 'way' of the soldier is to master the finesse of his weaponry. It is important for the soldier to know the killing power of each weapon, as well as its limitations. Some soldiers are better in platoons where they can draw strength from others, some soldiers are better when left to fight on their own. It takes a special kind of person to like this 'way'.

Like the soldier and farmer the 'way' of the artist is to become proficient in the use of his tools. First he must formulate his idea and then perform his work according to his concept. The idea is only a dream of the artist until his skill is put to use and common items become transformed into objects of art. His blueprint is only a concept. His canvas is his creation, whatever form that may be.

Although this book is designed to help people wishing to sharpen their management skills it should be noted that there are many other professions which demand dedication to strategy and the 'way' of success. To succeed in one's profession by following the 'way' of strategy is to insure success in other fields as well. The basic laws ruling the 'way' of strategy are as basic to human nature as are the five elements which make up the Buddhist cosmos: Ground, water, fire, wind and void (nothingness, or illusion). These are the five basic elements supporting the existence of life as we know it.

It was said if you were to master the art of sword fighting, when you beat one person, you could beat any man in the world. That the spirit of defeating one man is the same as it would be for a million men. The spirit of closing a small sale has the same make up as the art of closing a big one. The spirit of conquering small problems is the same as it would be for overcoming much larger ones. A strategist makes small things into big things; what is big is easy to see, what is small is much harder to see. Remember it is easy for a single person to change his mind and therefore become unpredictable. It is more time consuming for a large group of men changing their minds, making their movements more predictable.

In a small business the owner is usually the manager and must make functional decisions daily. It is far easier for him to keep abreast of the trends because he has only to acknowledge the trend is taking place. The corporation, however, must have a board meeting and try to get a majority of people to agree in principle. Flexibility is important to good management, and reflexive thinking is mandatory to good judgment. The ability to get ahead of the competition may rest on the fact that you are able to make on-the-spot judgments rather than going through a committee. You should appreciate this concept and practice always the ability to make quick decisions. An irrational decision is not mean a quick decision.

Have you ever watched a person practicing "Tae Kwan Do?" If you have, you may have noticed that the practitioner of his martial art, as others, goes through a routine of prepared movements. These ingrained movements take the place of having to think during battle. By having a repertoire of movements engraved in your mind, you need only react to a situation rather than think it through. In time of combat this could save your life. So it is in the 'way' of strategy. You must have a series of prepared responses to the most common questions or situations. When you do, you will find many of those prepared responses are based on tradition.

For example, when someone asks, "How are you?" your reflex response is "Fine, and yourself?" You do not stop to list any current ailments, or problems with your spouse or the bank. You simply say, "Fine." Similarly, it is the 'way' of management. When certain problems with customers or employees arise there are basic answers that are put into place almost immediately.

In the interest of good management there must be some initial quick response. This shows the customer, as well as the employee, that the manager is in charge, the situation has been recognized and is being dealt with. If the situation develops into a far more complicated one than first thought, at least the machinery to solve that type of problem is in place. This gives the manager time to re-evaluate the task at hand and make whatever mid-course corrections he deems necessary.

All this is done while the customer and employee are seeing positive reaction from management. This develops trust and is ground work for confidence. No leader can be successful without these two basic characteristics. If enough trust and confidence have been compounded over the history of the manager, then should the time arise where a crisis situation develops, the chances are good that the employee will follow the manager without question, much like the platoon leader who commands respect of his troops while leading them into battle.

"All roads lead to Rome." At least they did centuries ago. There are many roads to Rome, but not all of them are direct. There can only be one shortest way. Some roads may have detours and others may be undesirable because of the nature of their design. So it is that the 'way' to strategy is filled with side roads and off ramps. If you take time to study a 'way' every day and you diverge, you may think you are not studying a good 'way' when you are not following the true 'way'. The 'way' of strategy is the 'way' with nature. When you can appreciate the power of nature and know the rhythm of any given situation you will very likely come up with the best decision for success.

chapter 2

I REMEMBER A very old story about three blind men who will illustrate another point on how to study the 'way'.

Once upon a time, many years ago, there were three blind men who were invited to a circus. They were led hand in hand to the area where the elephants were kept. Then they were turned loose and told to 'see' the elephant. Each man wandered carefully to where the elephant stood tied.

The first touched the elephant by his trunk. "Oh," he said, "this animal is strong and rough and feels like a large leather pipe."

"He feels more like a large leather wall." said the second man who had walked into the side of the mammoth creature.

"You are both wrong," replied the third, who was holding the elephant by the tail, "he feels more like some strange kind of rope."

Because they were blind and could only see by touch, they were each right as they described the elephant based upon their touch; but they failed to 'see' the entire animal. If you view a problem by only studying the parts and not the whole, you will fail to understand the nature of the problem. This will cause recommending solutions for parts of the problem rather than addressing the overall problem. Not recognizing the situation as a whole may create an even larger problem. When faced by a puzzling situation, first stand back for a moment and become calm. When you become calm even complex events can appear less complicated, becoming even more so the more open and receptive you become. This is a fundamental of the 'way'.

The 'way' dictates that you find the center and work your way out from there. To find a balance you must solve the situation from the center. This is to prevent the trap of solving only one area and ignoring the whole of the problem.

It is true that the whole problem, based upon complexities, may not be solved at one time, and each solution must have a beginning. If we reduce our scope to only one area we allow other areas to fester and risk losing control of them. However, if we address the whole while attending to the parts then the problem becomes more solvable.

We all have areas in which we excel and these are usually based upon the laws of human nature, the ones we address first. So it is when addressing a management problem, we are prone to work in the areas of our strengths first. If a professional golfer were to use only a favorite club when playing golf, and not the twelve or thirteen clubs in his bag, his golf score would suffer. Therefore he chooses the club appropriate to the situation and works from there. In fact, he may play an entire round and never use his favorite club, or the club in which he has the most confidence, if the appropriate lie is not evident. It is the selection of his clubs, his knowledge of his tools that allows the golfer to exercise a choice of decisions. So it is with the 'way' of management. We must use our skills as they are called upon and not fit the situation to our skills. If you fail to look at things on a large scale it will be difficult for you to master the 'way' of strategy. If you study these principles and become proficient with them, you will be able to work on and solve a multitude of problems at the same time.

A superior manager will manage many subordinates dexterously while conducting himself correctly, and maintain business profitably at the same time. For the manager who understands how this process works uses as little force as possible with people. He knows when force is used, conflict and argument usually follow. Therefore he uses a light touch, leading by guidance and example rather than by directive. It is not unusual for a new manager to come upon the challenge of a new position, and in order to show the employees he means business, produces an avalanche of new policy changes, with his name in large print at the bottom over the word "MANAGER".

chapter 3

RULES AND REGULATIONS weren't written to help managers, rather they were written to help the employee realize the parameters of the work area. Rules let the employee know what will and will not be tolerated. The 'way' of management is not to set forth needless rules and over-burden the employees with endless memorandums, but to be explicit in exactly what the goal is and qualify the standards by which the finished product will be accepted. Employees were hired because they possess certain skills which prove valuable to the manager. The 'way' of the manager is to help each employee display these talents in a manner benefiting the company. This will also help the employee gain pride and self-confidence so he will continue to do his best. The manager who pays equal attention to everything does so without prejudice, which would divide the workforce into factions. Terms like "Teacher's pet," or similar terms are in opposition to the 'way'.

By revealing to his employees the problems of the situation, the manager is helping them gain an awareness of the situation so they, in turn, may use their talents to best help solve the problem. The 'way' of the manager is to keep a positive appearance at all times when communicating with the employees, and never show negative emotions. Employees are much like a flock of feeding birds, if you approach the field of birds too quickly and directly, they will fly away in a disorganized manner, flapping their wings wildly and making unusual noises. If you remain calm and walk closer to the birds without walking directly at them, making them feel as if they are not the target of your approach, you can get much closer. When dealing with your employees remember not to be tense, nervous, or reckless, rather let your body relax; working always from within. Do not let your spirit slacken.

If you merely read this book without pondering the written word you will not reach the 'way' of management. You must do more than read, memorize, or imitate. The principles must come from within your own heart. Study to absorb these things into your being so they will become second nature to you. Then you will react properly and you will know the 'way'. You will develop an inner awareness, a sense of purpose in the 'way'.

A very important aspect of the 'way' is your spiritual well being. Both in business and in everyday life your reactions should be determined through inner calm. Meet situations without tenseness. Remember not to let your spirit be influenced by your body. Let your body influenced by your spirit. Do not let your employees see your emotions. Be unbiased in their behalf. Be poker-faced. Remember it takes intelligence to know how other people behave but to know yourself takes wisdom. Managing other peoples' lives takes great strength, but to manage your own life takes true power.

You must study people, all people, study them when they are happy and when they are not. Learn what makes them laugh and what their values are so you can use that knowledge to inspire them to reach their own level of greatness. Learn their level of honesty, and to what level a person will go to deceive while trying to avoid getting caught. Armed with this knowledge you can manage a person without their knowing.

The 'way' of the manager is to know when you cannot be deceived by man you will have realized the wisdom of strategy. To do this you need to develop a two-fold gaze, one of 'perception' and one of 'sight'. 'Perception' is for seeing, while 'sight' is merely for looking.

When a person comes to you for work and says, "Hire me," you will see his best side. No one comes to you for work acting less than what he thinks you are looking for in an employee, knowing if he does he will not get hired. However, once you have agreed to put him on the payroll then his other side comes out and you are left to manage him or fire him. Both take your valuable time. It's time that could be better used on the whole rather than the part. As you grow you will need to develop peripheral vision to see what the applicant is selling you on his own behalf, and comprehend what he is saying so you may know what questions to ask that will bring out the true nature of the applicant. This ability cannot be learned quickly. However with constant practice, as with anything, you will develop skills deep within yourself and know when to draw upon them. This is the 'way' of the manager, this is a law of strategy.

To manage from strength is to manage from within. The manager who is in control from within has the greatest advantage. There are always those special employees who will study the manager to know what is to be expected during a given situation. Based on repeated past performances by their manager, the employee can react almost prematurely to the whims of their manager. The manager who shows no emotion and does not respond similarly in like circumstances keeps his employees on their guard. Habits can be costly, versatility demands respect. You must demonstrate flexibility so that you and not the employee will be in charge of the situation.

According to history, in the early days of the United States, when the frontiersmen were in battle with British Redcoats, the Red Coats maintained a rigid single file attack structure against their American counterparts, who were hiding behind rocks and trees and other obstacles so as not to be shot. Consequently, because there was no flexibility in the pattern from the British the American frontiersmen found their enemy an easy target. Understand the meaning sleeping beneath the surface, it is the 'way' to insight.

Do not be confused with words already written. I have suggested to you to learn words and responses to facilitate a quick response, perhaps leading you to falsely think that once memorized, a handful of knowledge could write a brilliant future. One answer will serve one question. The martial arts practitioner must know many movements. The more you have committed to memory the better your response and the more quickly you will reach a positive solution to a myriad of situations.

When going head to head with an opponent of equal strength feign a weakness. This weakness must be based on your greatest strength, so that when your adversary tries to take advantage of you, he will walk instead into your strength. Deal from inner calm least you get restless and make errors in judgment that could jeopardize you and your business.

If you find someone in your organization, or from without, who challenges you remember to never seek a confrontation. If it comes to you, first step back and see your limitations rather than rush forward and overstep them. Your inner strength is your intelligence. Advance only where you find no resistance and score your point. Do not lavish the small victory or else you may get caught off guard and lose the match. This is the 'way' of strategy. You must also remember; the person who initiates the attack is off balance, and in life as in martial arts the attacker is more easily thrown. Always respect your challenger. It is far better to give him too much credit then not enough.

You may well face a challenge from a subordinate co-worker looking to change the system and increase his benefits. It may in turn come from another manager who is jealous of the good job you are doing and your position with the company. Thinking if he overcomes you in a confrontation he will then win respect for having beaten you. In matters of judgment no one knows everything. You are far wiser when you come to realize there are many things you do not know. You will gain much respect when you simply say, "I do not know!" The other choice would be to fake a good guess and hope that you are right, and if not, face the embarrassment of having humiliated yourself. You may think that because an employee is challenging your position on a directive or goal he is being disrespectful. Remember, employees are not fluent in the art of tactfulness and what may appear as confrontational may be the only way the employee has of introducing his point of view to you.

chapter 4

THERE IS NEVER a good time to discuss religion. The wise manager following the 'way' of strategy knows he must be willing and able to speak about the traditional values of religion, and also overcome the bias he will almost certainly find against the word "God". While researching different books on the art of managing, I have found a simple rule for success. A common thread to many books dating back to the early days of recorded time: "You can succeed at anything you want to in life as long as it does not defy the laws of God or man."

Like it or not our spiritual roots lie in tradition and all our being is centered from within, from the soul. The "God" I refer to is a non-denominational "God". He belongs to no one club or religious sect. He is the reason all that is, is, and He is responsible for the creation as we know it today and as the world will find it centuries from now. "God" does not appear weekly at places of worship to preach sermons to us or dictate our behavior. What people do is a result of their own free will. The pattern of their behavior follows natural law. "God" does not decide for you how to react to any given situation, it is up to you.

The 'way' of the manager is to meditate whenever he needs guidance; to return to his inner self and concentrate on the project at hand. To know the 'way' you must reach your mind and body strategy, taking your time to be complete. Today is a victory over yourself. Tomorrow is a victory over others. In order to beat men more skilled, you must train according to the 'way' and do not allow yourself to be sidetracked. Judge yourself by the same standards you judge others; do not judge yourself by another man's measure. The 'way' is the standard measure for all men.

Remember always where your strength comes from. Like the eye of a hurricane, the greatest strength lies at the center. As the winds nearest the center are the strongest and the winds at the perimeter the weakest, so it is with people. All strength, physical and spiritual, emanate from the center of oneself. A fighter's greatest punch is the short jab, the punch closest to the body. While an extended punch may have sufficient power to damage an opponent, maybe knocking him out, at the end of the reach there is less force because the energy is fading.

The snake, which coils and awaits its prey, stays coiled tightly, knowing the exact range of his lunge. When its victim comes within this invisible circle the snake watches its movements, measuring its speed and path. When the snake is certain of the direction of its prey it uncoils with a lightning-like strike then re-coils to the center. Nature has taught the snake there is strength from the center. From the center it can visually watch all sides at once, so it won't be taken by surprise. When the manager or leader gets so busy that he loses his perspective, then he should return to the center of the silence of meditation, rather than rant and rave at the ways of the world; trying to solve problems from amid them. It is time to regroup. Meditation brings one to his center; from the center we find order, and with order the solutions become more obvious.

Skeptics of the easy road through life, those looking for simple solutions by default say, "If man is to only seek benefit from those things that are easily within his grasp, he will not grow. Man must set his goals at some distant point. A point just beyond his grasp." Herein lies a valuable lesson. Learn it well. As the snake that waits patiently for that final moment when he will uncoil and strike, it must be remembered, the snake will follow his prey for some time until he is ready to attack under his own conditions. After he has picked out his victim he will circle around and position himself in the course he thinks his prey will be likely to follow. He will only attack when the conditions for success are in his favor.

So it is with the 'way' of management and of big business. The corporation looking to buy out the weaker or less powerful company cannot divulge its purpose too early in negotiations or else the price may go up, or it might even put the company on guard to a point where it would be taken off the market. Instead, the corporation should look like it is considering many other small companies, giving the one it really wants only token attention. This will take the focus from the corporations intended goal allowing for an easier take-over when all the parts are in place and the surprise choice is made to the public.

If they see you coming, they have time to move out of the way, or at least impede the progress by setting up roadblocks and taking evasive actions which may frustrate your original purpose. Remember the 'way'. You must use your strengths at your opponent's weaknesses in order to gain advantage.

Remember also to use this philosophy as it applies to groups of people, both large and small. The wise manager then determines the goal for the group, and when the final or main goal is set firmly in your mind, find as many smaller goals as you can that will send you in the same direction as your ultimate goal. Explain your ultimate goal to your employees, but do not labor the point because many employees get frustrated readily when a goal is set to far ahead of them. They can, however, understand more simple and direct goals.

When each small goal is reached a victory must be celebrated. This gives co-workers incentive to reach the next goal while bolstering morale and ego. People always feel better when they have accomplished something positive. Do not let them fail, especially if the ultimate goal is a long way down the road. Co-workers generally have lesser vision and, like unherded sheep, will wander in many different directions taking more valuable time to turn them around and refocus them later down the road. As each smaller goal is reached the workers will begin to expect to succeed and become more self-motivated as they work towards the completion of yet another goal.

The hunter who baits his trap with food also leaves a trail of food down a path towards his trap. As the animal eats the food he follows the easy trail left behind by the hunter and eventually eats his way into the hunter's trap. So it is with employees. Lead them towards the final goal by letting them enjoy many small victories along the way, thus not letting the employees' goal exceed their grasp. All the while the vision of management is focused on a specific goal and their direction is being controlled from the center.

There is yet another valuable lesson for having many small victories or goals to be reached while guiding a work force towards some future point in time.

As the winds change constantly, sometimes devastatingly so, you must realize that your goal will most probably not stand still either. Therefore, remember, as you grow and learn and experience self-realization, your goals also change. You must be flexible in your thinking. Be able to make mid course changes in order to keep yourself on target. Remember this because it applies to everyday life, this is the 'way', learn it well.

In order to win at life you must take time and learn acceptance. Be patient and attack your problem at its weakest point. Put yourself in a position of advantage. Remember to return to your inner self to meditate in times of stress or indecision. From the center you can go in any direction. Once you have left the center the only way you can go is back.

A manager, of a few or many, must choose his goals and direction carefully. The people who depend on him for direction need to have the confidence of success. If too many mid-course corrections are needed to reach the goal then it could be said that insufficient time was spent in preparing the original plan.

Never be afraid to make changes; fearing those who follow you will think you are weak and do not know the way, and therefore not follow you with confidence. Do, however, make change in such a manner as to show those in your charge that the changes you are preparing to make are for the benefit of the group and will ultimately make achieving the goal a more realistic one. Although making too many changes may show weakness or indecision, making no decision is a far greater weakness, indicating a lack of understanding. As a sail boat must tack back and forth across the waters, fighting winds and currents, so the leader must make corrections, showing his understanding of the complex nature of his task and soliciting support from those under his command. Those who change direction with resolve are respected, but those who change because of distress are feigned.

One corporation looking to overtake another must spend the time necessary to understand the disposition of the target company. Observe their capacity for work and the attitude of the work-force. If the productivity is lacking, perhaps it is due to a work-force of non-motivated workers. If sales are down perhaps it is because the sales force is not presented with proper incentives, or perhaps the product is inferior to the market place and competition or lacks consumer interest because of outdated benefits. Once the strong company sets its sights on the target company, it cannot let go. Its instincts tell it to pursue, dealing from strength to take whatever advantage it can. Do not let them recover, but do not destroy them in the take-over. Beware, you could cause permanent damage, defeating the reasons for the take-over.

Never underestimate an opponent, and knowing the 'way'. Never talk yourself out of a victory by giving your target too much credit. If you know the 'way' of strategy, then, be like the chess master who waits patiently for the opponent to make a careless move so he can gain only one square on the chess board, knowing that in the end he will surely win by controlling the game. Do not push your opponent into making a defeating move, if in doing so, you would have to move off center. Allow your opponent to make a bad move by giving him too much room. If he encounters no opposition, he will surely seek it, and when he is sufficiently off center, you may make your move from strength and prevent his returning. Remember, in taking over a company, the principles of strategy are the same as taking over a position of leadership, only the target changes.

The chess master, in order to gain control, may deem it necessary to sacrifice a pawn or some other piece to bait a trap and eventually win his opponent's queen or capture his king. By what would appear to be a weak move and allowing your piece to be taken, you have gained momentum and can move your other pieces to their proper squares. If your opponent has taken the bait then he is out of sync with his own game plan and will have trouble retreating. Now you have momentum on your side, you will have the timing to make things happen. Once you capture this momentum keep it, because timing is all important in a close encounter.

In a game of chess, as in the game of life, if you have the opponent agitated so he shows an inclination to rush, do not mind, instead be calm. Strength comes from the center; from the calm of inner peace. If the opponent is rushing to beat you he is off balanced and can be easily tripped. If you yawn in his presence and create in him the need to yawn also, then you know he is in your control, and subject to your power of suggestion. If, however, he looks you in the eye and smiles, you must know that he is in complete control of his thoughts and his body. This should cause you to recoil, like the snake, and proceed with caution. If your opponent is equally strong in thought and is as well prepared in rhetoric, you must move to knock him off balance. If the opponent is a corporation, an unruly employee, or a logistical problem, the 'way' of the solution is fiercely similar.

Perhaps to get your opponent off balance you must throw him into a state of confusion. Again, like the chess master who is playing a student of the game who has mastered the principles of the openings, the master may make a move that is in none of his books, only to make the opponent think he knows some attack totally alien to his opponent. Thus confusing him and causing him to doubt his own ability. The master will, even if he makes a blunder, present the move in such a way as to let his opponent think it was a well planned move, with traps and danger waiting only a few moves away. This will cause the opponent to spend much time researching the move to determine it was only a fluke, and throw him off his game plan.

Remember, the 'way' of management is to have a game plan and follow it as closely as possible. Albeit vague at first, it may only be to know that, "Here I am, and the goal I seek is over there." Once the goal is realized, the strategy for reaching the goal can be formulated. You can do this only by knowing your pieces. As the chess master knows the value of each piece on the board, so must the manager know the strength and value of those he is leading. You must have the right co-worker performing the task for which he is best suited; if the goal is to be reached with the least effort.

Imagine if you will that the coach on a football team needs only a field goal to win a game. He surly wouldn't let his best cheer leader kick the field goal, nor would he be likely to let his quarterback kick the field goal. If he wants the highest degree of possible success he would let the field goal kicker kick the field goal. Managers must know their team, know their strengths, weaknesses, and breaking points.

This is most important. Know just how far you can push your employees in their given tasks to help you reach your goal. If you have a weak team and you take them to task you are asking for failure. This failure is sure to demoralize what good players you may have. Keep the right players, or co-workers, in their right position. Know when to shift the weight of the project to another area or co-worker so as not to overburden anyone. Shout your orders with energy and authority. Arouse those who follow, wake up their spirits and they will repay you with hard work.

chapter 5

AT SOME TIME during our lives, we have all been the subject of attack. It would be very unlikely that anyone would go through life and not be the victim of an attack. Be it personal, business related, political or spiritual. Even an attack on a family member, justified or not, can be a cause for great concern.

The spirit of attacking another person, a problem, or a goal is not so very different than it is to be attacked. It is very unlikely anyone would go through life and not be a victim, whether it is personal, business related, political or spiritual. The same energies and emotions we felt during the attack can be used to turn the advantage to our favor and achieve a productive goal. Whether you are the subject of another company's desired takeover, or if the employees have clearly turned against your leadership, you will benefit by following the basics to the 'way' of strategy.

Remember the snake. Recoil, do nothing. Go within and evaluate the situation. Show no emotion until you get your bearings and an understanding for the circumstances. If, while evaluating the situation you are attacked, it is important for you to feign a weakness. This will give the attacker a target for his vengeance and should allow you time to regroup as you are back peddling. The weakness you show your adversary should be built on your strength.

Determine what the target of the attack is about. Was it caused by an action, or was it due to lack of action. Perhaps you terminated someone's job or failed to give a promised promotion. In a political situation you may have been targeted as a weak link and a way in for your opponent.

If your company is under attack because of a hostile takeover you must be quick to find out what reserves you have to fight with and what your legal limits are. Perhaps you can divert the part of your business that has drawn interest and sell it off to a concerned third party, or at least tie it up in the process of a sale (by taking it off the market) until it is safe to break off negotiations.

If the attack you are under is the more commonly found type, one of stress, which can in itself be devastating, remember the story of oak tree and the storm. After a severe storm has gone by, one accompanied by high winds, go about the streets and roads where large oak trees grow. The oak, while strong and the symbol of might, even though it came from humble beginnings, does not have the same type of strength as the willow. While the willow is not mighty nor does it give the appearance of strength, it possesses a great quality the mighty oak does not. After the storm you will notice that there are branches missing from the oak, because the oak stands tall and firm in the face of adversity. A macho, or perceived masculine thing to do by society. The willow, not bearing the characteristics of strength inherent to the oak, in order to survive the adversities of life, has learned the lesson of being flexible. Bending in the face of adversity.

Think, if you will, of a large open window in a room covered with venetian blinds. Suppose the blinds are fastened to the top of the window and tied to the bottom. When the blinds are turned so that the blades are in a horizontal position, the light and the view outside can be seen. Now, if we close the blinds, keeping out the light and the wind, we see nothing. However, if a strong wind blows against this open window while the blinds are in the closed position, the blinds will billow like a sail on a boat in a storm. If the attacking winds are serious and sufficiently strong for any duration against the closed blinds, the pressure on the blinds will cause them to become loose and fall, or be blown into some form of disrepair.

A wise person, seeing the stress building up against the blinds will adjust them to the open position allowing the winds of adversity in, but also saving the blinds from destruction. Being strong is no great feat if you are knocked down trying to hold your ground. So, it may be said, by giving into the stresses of life, at certain times, and allowing the stress to flow through you like winds through an open blind, you have a better chance of regaining your position and your balance. Keeping your balance and standing upright can be done more easily if you have not been dismembered like the oak trying to hold your ground. Standing tall and firm in the face of adversity may simulate a false sense of pride. It does, however, represent an arrogance of ignorance of the whole, sacrificing the short term for the duration.

Stress is an unfortunate state of being. Much stress can be alleviated by meditation. Meditation is the universal catalyst to self control, willpower and the manifestation of ego. Other forms of stress can be far more damaging than the winds of a great storm.

You must train yourself to know when you are in a period of stress and picture in your mind the open blinds, allowing the stress to pass. For many years I have learned to picture in my mind a great oak on the top of a hill overlooking the sea. When the winds of stress begin to attack, I picture the mighty oak standing firm and in my mind's eye I see the oak starting to bend. Then I see the branches of the oak open up, allowing the winds to pass through so that only a few leaves are blown loose.

You can teach your body to act like a thermostat so that when your subconscious feels the invasion of stress it will automatically flash a picture of an open blind in your mind. I do not mean to say that by merely memorizing this simple exercise that stress will no longer be a factor in your life. However, like a fighter in the ring sensing a punch about to be thrown at him, he is able to duck, weave, and bob his head, so even if he is hit, the full intensity of the blow will not be felt. The same applies to the stress of being attacked. The 'way' of strategy applies here also.

Some stress, like the daily kind, such as the alarm that awakens you in the morning, or the unexpected phone call in the middle of the night that awakens you abruptly, is to be expected. Getting caught in a traffic jam on the way to work and being late for an early morning appointment can also be anticipated. All these are daily doses of stress and our bodies have a built in defense mechanisms. Some of us groan and mutter "Not again!", and some of us say more prolific things. In any case these verbal utterances are all means of venting frustration and getting our stress levels under control. In more difficult situations throwing dishes against the wall may be the path taken. Other people choose to exercise, which is probably the most beneficial. It burns off negative energy and doesn't hurt anyone.

Take a deep breath, close your eyes and take three long deep breaths; after each breath, hold it in your lungs for a ten count, and then let it out slowly. You may experience some dizziness, or see spots before your eyes, but you need the oxygen, and it helps to relax you and purge your body of stress.

Someone far greater than I once said that for every action there is a reaction. Even when doing a good deed the response may not be favorable. Remember to duck, weave, and retreat to your center. Do not mix words with lesser men merely to beat them and show your superiority. Nod your head instead, acknowledge their presence and go on to more important things.

chapter 6

THE 'WAY' OF management is filled with setbacks, side-tracks, and humor. It is the humor that can be found in almost any situation that is cause and fuel for doing a better job. A personal friend of mine and a very good manager in his own right was telling me of an incident with his new assistant manager: He managed a very large national department store with annual sales in excess of 12 million dollars. He had two assistants and several trainees. His newly promoted assistant, high strung by nature and very nervous with his newly acquired responsibilities, was constantly making mistakes because he was trying too hard. One night around midnight this manager was awakened by a phone call from his now frantic assistant manager. It seems that he had locked the door to the safe while it was open, and now he could not get the door closed. He had the day's deposit on his desk as well as the change banks for twelve registers. What was he to do?

I suppose at midnight, when a not so funny near disastrous situation is unfolding, we sometimes forget the 'way'. The usually tactful manager took a more direct not so tactful approach to solving the problem so that he could get back to sleep. He reminded the assistant that in order to get the money out of the safe in the first place he had to have opened the door. He told the assistant to dial the combination and when the tumblers unlocked the safe he could then close the door. He later told me that he now understood the term "The silence was deafening". Being a manager may at times put you to a test by less than talented assistants, or employees who seem to provoke a situation.

I remember reading a story from a restaurant journal some years ago that may better illustrate this point. A traveling businessman went downstairs to the restaurant located in the hotel, in which he was staying, to order his dinner. An elderly waitress approached him somewhat disgruntled. It was late at night, just before closing and she had started doing her side work when the customer had interrupted her. Rather than asking if she could help him, she said, "What do you want?"

"What is tonight's special?"

"A Delmonico." she said tersely.

"How big is it?" he asked.

"Why, what are you going to do with it, eat it or weigh it?"

I would like to think that this story isn't true. Since it came from a reputable magazine, it probably is.

How about the employees who are always running four or five minutes late every day. They come rushing into work, punch in, and then run to the restroom to finish getting dressed. Fifteen minutes later they appear ready to go on coffee break. Why not! How do you apply the 'way' to these situations?

The waitress, of course, needed to be terminated. Some types of management situations do not leave room for discussion, nor for tactful ways to promote better service. Where blatant displays of arrogance are allowed to take place and continue, there is no virtue in management. The disciplinary action for this type of behavior must be apparent when an employee is first hired. All companies should have a printed form with rules and regulations. This will not make the employee work harder, but will let him know the guidelines for behavior and any specific dress codes, etc. These rules will also contain specific disciplinary actions the employee can expect should he choose to violate them.

The manager with the assistant who locked the safe open took his assistant to lunch the next day. After a brief and embarrassing apology, both men laughed at the experience. I suppose that after midnight it can be harder to recoil to the inner self, especially when the inner self is still asleep.

Companies with large numbers of employees all know the frustration of having the great employee and the not so great. Both usually seem to get treated equally, however, the lesser employee seems to get away with more. At least he seems not to get caught. When the better employee does something sloppy his superiors seem to be more ready to bring it to his attention.

We have a tendency as managers not to deal with employees who are constant sources of problems or frustration. Again it bears repeating, if you want some-thing done, check on it. You can never over-check a project. Be ever so mindful of the scope of the proj-ect and the people who are executing it. It is a good practice for a contractor to visit with the laborers of his project asking them if they are having any trouble with supplies and then checking the value of their work. This is also done in order to keep up morale on the job.

I know of a factory president who had almost 500 employees and knew the majority of them by name. I was visiting one of them one day when we passed the president going down the hall and the president said, "Good morning Jim." This really impressed me and cer-tainly made Jim feel more important.

Remember also, the 'way' of managing, if you have a job to do that requires you to hire someone, the person doing the job is an important member of the team,. no matter what the job description. There have been songs written about people who have jobs others don't want. Because these people have a good self-im-age and a positive attitude, they will be the best at what they are doing no matter what. I remember a country song about a street sweeper who liked to sing while he was cleaning the street. That was the job he wanted to do, and he wanted to do a good job, because his integ-rity wouldn't let him settle for less.

I once interviewed a cab driver in a small Florida town. He knew all the history of the town and was very helpful about recommending a good place to eat and where the local places of interest were. I found out that he had a master's degree in mathematics and had taught college. After fifteen years he retired to drive a cab because that is what made him happy. There are many other stories I can relate with the same basic message. Rather than belaboring the point, I would rather refine the message. There is a biblical passage that goes something like this, "What good would it do a man to gain the whole world and lose his soul?"

I do not mean to be religious here, but the point is strong. Why should a person work hard every day at a job or profession that he really doesn't like just because it pays well or because it is all he knows. It may be all he knows really well, but the person knows himself and if he is not satisfied with his position in life then he is not putting forth his best effort and is not being true to his employer as well as himself. Ulcers and all sorts of disorders arise from placing yourself under unnecessary stress and forcing yourself to get up each day to face a challenge that causes you distress.

It is far better to come home after putting in a long stressful day filled with the knowledge that you have done a good job. Self satisfaction is a main ingredient to success. Can we measure success by the number of homes a person owns or the cars they drive? Hardly! Success is measured in the accomplishments of personal goals. The more goals a person can set for himself and then reach the more successful he is. Take pride in yourself, and it will reflect in the work you do. You cannot take pride in doing something you dislike or feel is beneath you. Even if the job is only temporary, put your all into it and make it a shining example of who you are.

W.J. "Duke" Mader

Over the course of a lifetime you may get laid off from work, for whatever reason. This in turn may lead to having to make a career change, or seeking reentry into the same field of work at a lower level than you had previously reached. There is stress in this and perhaps a personal feeling of having failed somewhere along the way. Certainly here is a substantial amount of balancing of the budget and discarding many of those well-deserved creature comforts. Life can deal cards that are all jokers at times, and for some of us it seems that this rut of insecurity only gets deeper the harder you try to climb out.

Failure can be a form of advancement for many people without their knowing it. For example take the laboratory scientist who fails many times while trying to perfect a formula. It would be great if they could just come up with an idea and make it work on the first try. The inventor must remake or redesign his idea countless times in order to make it work. We apply the same rule of life to the person who has been discharged, or laid off, as we do to the scientist who fails. Each time he tries to produce his anticipated end result and fails he finds out much about himself and his idea. He is forced to learn more about the chemical properties and their interaction each time he tries to mix a new batch. He cannot force the chemicals to interact in the manner that he needs to complete his project, so he must learn patience and carefully study the idiosyncrasies and other properties, sometimes filling volumes with learned observations. This does not ensure the experiment will ever be a success.

If after the scientist has spent sufficient time trying to perfect his formula, and it still does not work, he must take into consideration that his approach to the problem may not be the right one and that he will have to discard the project and try a whole new approach. So in effect he has laid himself off. However, over the term of the project he has learned enough about his work to know certain shortcuts or at least different starting places. Knowing what to do or not to do is a valuable tool.

So it is with the unemployed individual. He has working knowledge of his profession or occupation, and if he cannot find a lateral position at similar compensation, then he must deal with starting a new career. He must determine to which careers his job skills will most easily transfer. Also, if he is aggressive enough then he can package himself and his potential and go about and sell himself. If he chooses to re-enter the same field at a lower position and if his skills are adequate, then his rapid advancement in his new company is almost assured. No company will keep a talented employee in a position where he cannot exercise full use of his talents. Monetary compensation can be negotiated, "If I can do this for you, then I need, or expect you to do this for me."

Knowing these things doesn't take the sting out of being laid off or terminated. Remember the main rule of the 'way'. Recoil and seek strength through inner peace. Do not recoil to your inner sanctum and lock yourself in. The mind can be a most cruel hostage taker. The mind echoes fears and cries in such a way that no one hears. But the sounds to the person locked inside are deafening, and never ending. Be kind to yourself, it should be a personal commandment. As the farmer cannot blame himself for a lack of rain and the ensuing loss of a crop after much labor, neither should the worker, or manager blame himself for the lack of work, unless it was the result of a violation of man's or God's law.

I do not wish to make light of being terminated, or to make it sound like being terminated will enable a person to come out better than they started. Do not let the bitterness which always accompanies such actions poison you for the rest of your life.

chapter 7

IT IS MORE enjoyable to manage talented individuals than marginal ones. Those with talents can usually follow directions and have enough pride to see a task to completion. The ego is the main reason for doing almost anything according to Freud.

The 'way' of the leader is not to make a show of greatness or to pass out grades for effort. This would create a climate for success or failure in the work place. An emphasis on material success is much the same. It creates a climate for greed and avarice. Those with little become thief like, seeking whatever means come their way to "get", not "obtain", more. The 'way' of the manager is not to have favorites; otherwise, people will do anything to become recognized. The wise manager must pay attention to all behavior. Co-workers will work for the good of the goal and not the leader, if this lesson is followed.

The 'way' of the manager is to represent substance and not style, for the impression of success is not as long standing as creating from one's center. You will discover that the down-to-earth worker can do what needs doing more effectively than the person who is merely busy.

The 'way' of the manager is not to protect people from themselves. Because the light of justice and fairness shines equally on those things pleasant and unpleasant. If an employee has committed a violation of policy, and even if both you and the co-worker know of this breach of trust, fairness dictates that the employee be reminded of this act. The degree of intensity on the employee's part will dictate to what level the reprimand comes. A blatant act will require a far more firm action than one of negligence. If there are other co-workers who know of this act, you can be assured that they will be aware of the degree of the punishment handed down, especially if the co-worker in question is one who others would refer to as a "favorite". No one type of person is better than the rest of humanity. This same concept which underlies humanity also equates to everything else. God created everything equally. One person is as worthwhile as the next. Why should we play favorites? The 'way' of the manager is not to choose the person based on anything less than ability. Therefore, race, creed, or sex should not become a measure when trying to fulfill a goal. Unfortunately ever since the recording of time it has been apparent that the male of the species was in some way more dominant and his abilities inherently superior to women. There was a prominent psychiatrist I once interviewed who gave me much food for thought and enabled me to see things with a better perspective.

He said that if you were to test a male dock worker for yin and yang, his male attributes versus his female qualities, anima or animus, you would probably find the dock worker to score higher masculine attributes than a male teacher for example. The basic male dominated world is one of conquest based on strength and dominance over territory and the female. Take for examples, the rooster and his many hens, or the stallion and his mares. When we include the variable of knowledge we find that there is a melding of virtues and ideals. There is less of a need for identification based on sex, and a greater need for recognition based on accomplishment and ego. Wisdom or knowledge has no sex. Intelligence is a neutral substance. It can only be found in various degrees in the animal world. In some exotic birds it appears in the form of mimicry or simple tricks.

As we grow as a people we learn that true strength lies in the knowledge of oneself and of one's value to the completion of the cycle of this universe. Awareness comes with growth; as we learn who we are. We can then interpret who we are and how we are. This is a simple lesson but one that may never be learned. In our lifetime it involves going back to the beginning. It is like going back to one's center for the best view. If we do not understand the beginning, but only the part from where we entered life, then we can only work on the last half of the problem. To be a complete person we must know our beginning, and I am not referring to our heritage or our roots.

To learn yourself you must become open and receptive, quiet and without desires or the need to be doing something. Meditate on yourself being in a quiet valley with a pond. When there is no inner turmoil or distress, the waters of the pond will be mirror like. In this reflection you can see the face of God over your shoulder, and if you concentrate long and hard enough you can see creation. If you are in need of a place to go to solve problems go to the pond. Seek your answers in the reflection of the face of God. If you cannot see a reflection then it is because you are not sure of the question, or your motive is less than honorable, and you will never fool the pond. Troubled waters will always reflect the mood of the vessel that holds it.

Go into this valley as often as you wish. Be still and allow your fears and troubles to flow from your body. Concentrate on inner silence. With peace of mind comes tranquility. Your pond will never dry out. As you learn to grow back to your beginning you will know that the pond, and God, are within you always. You cannot go to them in panic and expect immediate answers. You must visit them on their terms. This is the 'way' to the beginning. Learn it well, practice it often, and each trip to the pond will take less time and become more consuming and virtuous.

The wise leader himself is like the water. Remember the function of water is to cleanse and refresh all creatures without distinction or judgment. So the leader works at his goal with any person or issue that appears. The leader acts so that all will benefit and he will work for their benefit no matter their rank or pay rate. The leader speaks so all that hear may understand. He is honest and works to create harmony among his workers. As water is yielding to the shape of its container, the leader is yielding to the circumstances of his surroundings. The 'way' of the leader is to create a need or a vacuum and let the employees fill it with their talents and job skills. It is like trying to push a rope. You cannot do it. However, pulling one requires a leader, someone who knows in what direction the rope should be going. If the leader is going in the right direction then all will reach their desired end. Each of us holds talents for which others will follow. All of us follow someone, or something daily. Be it a preconceived goal with detailed instructions for achievement, or the desire to follow someone with talents that will get us in the direction in which we want to go anyway.

Following takes the pressure of decision making away from the weaker and directly places more burden on the leader. If there is a mistake, then someone else is to blame, and "It's not my fault." The 'way' of the leader is to get all his followers to the end of the journey intact. It is also known that there will be those who give up no matter how great the leader. Some will quit during the course; others will find an off ramp or exit they wish to visit along the way. These people will never reach your goal. Do not feel it necessary to take these people under your wing of personal protection, for you will only feel overburdened and irritated at their lack of self interest.

chapter 8

MOST BOOKS ON management, or speakers who do moti-
vational speeches on the subject of management
principles, have code words or trick slogans that they
hang their speeches on. Many others have some sort
of mathematical formula, such as "Work times effort
equals expectation." or some such thing. Unfortunately
most people do not equate to numbers, nor will you
effectively motivate an employee by expressing that
they will best reach a goal by suggesting that they mul-
tiply their efforts by their expectations and have them
understand just what it is that you are trying to tell
them. The 'way' of the manager is to understand yourself so that you may understand others.

As you are an individual in the work force so
are the people both under your command and those
above you and your peers. All this can be labeled,
"Know thyself." Patterns, like code words and formulas
to maximize effort or productivity, are not going away.
As I have suggested earlier in this book, it is a good idea
to learn about other things along the 'way'- just do not

become sidetracked. There is no sure fire quick way to lose weight is as little as seven days. There is no such thing as a quick way to success in any field or endeavor. It would be naive of anyone to rely on their management capabilities based on some sort of code word that would represent a series of steps to be followed during times of stress or compromise.

The 'way' of the manager is not to seek any such inflexible standard, but to draw within, and then after getting a better understanding of the situation to go forward with natural decisions. The 'way' would never permit such basic "See spot run." logic rule a management situation. Any student of the 'way' will see some basic use for early training. However, the concepts are far too restrictive to be of any use in real management situations. I would not tempt the maturity of my readers to try and spell out some alphabetical magic to insure their success. It takes wisdom, fortitude, and a great desire to bear the burden and responsibility for others. This cannot be taught nor can it be learned. With a strong desire and a willingness to study, and study even more, and seek knowledge, it can be developed. For those who feel that they need greater compassion for their fellow man, they will tell you that awareness of mankind, its needs and expectations, are ongoing and ever tempting.

To expect that someone could take a few courses on how to win friends, or take the basic management entry level courses offered at a local college or university, and supplement that with a subscription to a management-based periodical expecting these things would make them a sufficiently talented manager, is of course foolhardy.

I suppose that it would be fair to say almost all people are born with an ability or instinct to be "bossy". This, however, is not the same as being "boss". Telling others what to do is the easy part, telling them how to do it is much harder. Telling them what to expect once they complete their task is even harder yet. To carry this one step further, being able to share their experience with them is the ultimate feeling of success for the manager. I should say one of the 'ultimate experiences', because there are certainly more than one. Sharing the feeling of accomplishment of a hard to reach goal and being able to relate to an employee an emotional concept, and then see it fall into place with a look of thanks from the employee for having told him what to expect is rewarding.

For those of you who are chastising me for using the term 'ultimate' while describing experiences and meanings, "the highest form of", indicating the one, and not one of the many, I say this: "The ultimate for me is certainly not the ultimate for others, and while their ultimate experience may be of little significance to me, others may relate well to it. Therefore, there are many ultimate experiences. When all of them are put together, and while each of us may only have what we consider one 'ultimate' experience, it would be unfair to say that the rest of these experiences were any less important.

There is nothing wrong with management seminars or workshops. Each teacher will profess his "Ideals" in a capsule program based on what works for them. Again most of these teachers are guided by one or two main themes and they base all their presentations on them. They also try to fit much of the management seeds into their mold, displaying their system as a catch-all problem solver, and if used religiously, will almost surely provide answers for the majority of the problems facing the student. Common sense dictates that one set of answers cannot be molded to fit all situations, no matter how flexible the mold. I believe that it is these teachers and lecturers who preach a system rather than the reality of the problem, and who are the greatest threat to the serious beginner or student. It is because of their flashy style of teaching and their use of gimmicks that are easily remembered or easily identifiable that make them dangerous. On the surface they seem to be in command of themselves and their subject, however their knowledge is strictly limited to their system which they will use to defend any question. These people are good to help you get started, if you remember the 'way' of management is far more on-going, and requires knowledge and wisdom far too superior to be confined to a boxed equation.

One of the better managers I have had time to interview over many years was a natural leader. He had charisma, charm and what could only be called a 'knack with people'. I asked him if he had a special book or a favorite person that he styled himself after. He had never gone to a management workshop and he said he got his best advice from listening to the people he managed. He was the manager of a national chain store with about two hundred people working for him. He knew all of them by name, and spoke to them whenever he passed them during the course of his daily routine.

As a matter of fact he was so good that the president of his corporation made a personal appearance to find out how he had remodeled two stores in two years and came in well under budget and way ahead of schedule. His simple answer was that he went to the stock room manager (who had many years with the company), the receiving clerk, and other department heads (who had been dealing with receiving and ticketing) for their input. He then went over the corporate schedule with them and asked their opinion as to whether or not it could be done. All of them agreed that it could be done, but not like it was drawn on paper. They drew up a new game plan and threw out the one from the home office. The manager was there fourteen hours daily overseeing the progress, sweeping the floor and adding words of encouragement where needed. It also helped that he had a great ego and didn't like to be second in anything. I might add this man had only a high school education and had worked his way up the ranks from the stock room. It has been said that if you wish to learn about canaries, you should study canaries. If you want to learn how to manage people, then study people.

Managing emotions, egos, pride and even a lack of these same attributes are all inclusive in studying the person. I have a small handmade plaque that was a gift many years ago that says, "Acceptance, the hardest lesson." We cannot mold people into easier to manage packages, so we must accept them for what they are and the situation for what it is. Then go from there.

If you have a strong desire to learn and a good memory, you can remember those important things you will study about people. You may become an effective manager without the help of books or management courses. This would certainly be the hard and long way. To study from other respected leaders and learn what tricks they use to keep things together or how they learned to managed people will bring about knowledge much faster and with a greater chance of success. Study the masters; they will show you the 'way'; they will not lead you to the elevator.

chapter 9

ONE OF THOSE things we all try to avoid is confrontation. We have them almost daily in some form or another. It can start with the waitress who forgets to bring us the sugar substitute in the morning, and we have to sit and wait for that first cup of coffee while our contemporaries are oohing with satisfaction with their cup, or when we're late and rush to get in the next elevator so we will get to work just in time and the door slams shut in our face. We can have a good employee who is having a bad week, personally or at work, or maybe even a bad month. Once we have had an initial meeting with the employee, usually trying to instill some enthusiasm and our concern about their situation, we try to express our desire to help and also to remind the co-worker that there is still work to be done. In most cases the employee may be under more stress than is apparent or facing some other major personal event that he has kept a secret from everyone.

It is usually the lesser-class employee that causes the most problems for the manager. This employee will challenge the authority of the manager and push his luck forcing confrontation with management. Rules are rules, and the 'way' of the manager is to enforce all policies as equally as possible and not show favoritism, lest lose the respect of the other employees. None of us like to be put in a situation where we are forced to take disciplinary action against anyone. Writing a report or having to take an employee aside and suspend or terminate them is usually something that we all do only as a last resort. Employees who become disenchanted with the system or who feel that they have been passed up for a promotion or raise, may become melancholy, lithesome and less productive than allowable. Measures must be taken as soon as these types of situations are recognized to show other employees that these rules are held in high regard by management and will be dealt with in an efficient manner.

If management is challenged by an employee to make an on the spot decision, like "Fire me!" in front of other employees, the situation becomes more volatile. This gives the employee a temporary advantage by putting management on the defensive, and makes the response of management even more meaningful, because there will be an immediate response by all the other co-workers. Employees being as they are will almost always side with their peers, those against management. Therefore, it is mandatory that management remembers the 'way' of strategy and does nothing immediately until he recoils within and observes the situation and can make a rational judgment without being intimidated. After taking a deep breath management should respond by saying something like "Let's continue this conversation in my office."

Whatever happens there is no need for an audience. It will be to the advantage of both people if their meeting takes place later in the day, or even the next day, thus allowing the two parties to cool off and become more rational. Management must take the initiative at some point, early on is best, and offer a solution. After allowing the employee to blow off steam and perhaps make a fool of himself, it is to the advantage of management to suggest a way out. If this is an event in a series of repeated performances by the employee, then a permanent arrangement is most probably in order. By coming up with a compromise, the dealing power is in the hands of management, it is their compromise, and will benefit both parties, but management is in charge. Based on the seriousness of the event and on its occurrences, management has many choices, from temporary suspension to the permanent termination.

Whatever happens leave the co-worker with his self-respect. Beating an employee down is never an answer. It is a form of revenge, and does no one any good. A manager who uses their position to punish an employee is wasting their authority. While the employee in question may have deserved to be punished, other co-workers will also realize and find abusive the use of retaliatory steps taken by management. Don't work to lose the respect of your employees by over stressing rules and regulations. Show leniency to a point, and then justice, dealt equally and expeditiously. Never drag out a situation. It will only get worse for management.

chapter 10

AMONG OTHER TALENTS the manager must have, or at least work to develop, is that of an artist. I do not mean the paint brush type. Although that would be beneficial, I am speaking about creating a scene with words. The manager must paint a vivid vision of the things to come, and how the things that are will change with the accomplishment of the goals set before everyone. These visions are important for any type of management.

The manager of a retail store, by setting realistic goals for the staff, can create an atmosphere of "best in the chain" with personalized rewards for top performers. The restaurant manager can instill better service from the wait-people by expressing a desire to see more positive customer response, which will in turn lead to a higher tip average. Even the gas station attendant can learn his regular customers by name. Just because we have "do-it-yourself" gas stations doesn't mean that we cannot provide better service. Remember that once upon a time gas stations were called "Service" stations.

Service is a main ingredient for positive customer feedback. That is to say good service usually results in good feedback, poor service in poor feedback. We work hard to see to it that a project is completed with a high degree of integrity. We should also instill that same degree of integrity in our employees.

We know that it would be foolish to expect one hundred percent from our employees, and we also know there is a point that we will accept less than one hundred percent. Likewise, there is also a point where we will not accept less than one hundred percent. Maximum efficiency is usually evident during times of crisis, times when it is critical for all personnel to perform the duty they were hired for. The trick is not to let the employees know where the line is drawn. For instance, if you expect one hundred percent but will settle for eighty-five percent, the employees will only exert eighty-five percent energy. That equates to eighty-five percent of the eighty-five percent you originally expected in the first place. Remember they are not able to perform one hundred percent. They can produce their normal output of eighty-five percent, so they cannot do eighty-five percent of one hundred percent, but eighty-five percent of eighty five percent. Confused? Remember that employees will always fall a little short of perfect, so by lowering their goal to their level, they will almost assuredly lower their output by the same amount.

Painting goals is only one aspect of the creative artist in all good managers. Painting the results of the achievements of these goals is also important. Show

how once the goals are accomplished raises, performance bonuses, or some form of gain can be realized by the participating co-workers. Painting goals that coincide with the accomplishment of the company goals is also important. Make the employee aware of the fact that his résumé will boast of his accomplishments and that this will surely help him if he is seeking to climb the corporate ladder. Show him how this will enable him to better provide for his family and to get those things he really wants out of life.

Many presidents of large corporations were once dishwashers and laborers. They did not start at the top, but in many cases worked hard from the bottom. The manager must learn the structure of the system. As he learns he grows. This gives him wisdom and much knowledge. It is then up to him to draw upon this wisdom and knowledge and use it for the benefit of those he represents.

Sometimes the artistic part of management must be called upon to draw the bitterness of reality for his co-workers. He must be able to express the seriousness of failure, if the common goal is not reached. That if the products that the company makes are inferior, the company will lose sales and this in turn will represent a loss of employees, or perhaps a freezing of wages, or a loss of benefits. It is for the good of the employee to see to it his company does well, and it is the 'way' of the manager to help him to see and understand this truth. This does not call for a manager to preach hell, fire and damnation for failure, but to preach the reality of the situation as it relates to the co-worker.

W.J. "Duke" Mader

It is necessary for management to paint an explicit picture to the employees and team leaders, so they may in turn pass on the images to the people they are responsible for. If the assistants are of sufficient quality, they will more readily comprehend those things being expressed by management and should be able to pass along the vision to their subordinates. Each person will have at some point a picture in their minds of what it is they are expected to do. If rewards or incentives are being passed along, these should be received with the same degree of intensity as the goal oriented values.

One of the better sources of employees is the high school. While high schools cannot distribute skilled co-workers to the labor market, they can give the work force something that they may not be able to get in other places. This is "Esprit De Corps", or team spirit. With most high schools having sports teams and cheerleaders, high schools are noted for pep rallies and positive attitudes for the home team. With good management this team spirit can be transferred to company spirit, and of course positive attitude can be contagious. Use this energy that high school students can bring to your business to energize the rest of your work force. When employees are proud of their job and their company they are more productive, there is less absenteeism, and the overall work ethic reflects in the company's products and public image.

The youth of any country are basically the same. They possess high ideals and an eagerness for the truth. They have a desire to create waves, not necessarily waves of resistance but waves of recognition. Waves that are created by someone splashing around in the work pool saying, "Hey, recognize me!"

These youth are full of exuberance, almost to the point of challenging the companies that they work for to do better and to be a standard for their own industry. While the youth have many fine attributes, they also have the rare quality of the maverick stallion: strength, speed, independence, and are hard to train, not impossible to train. For the most part they are very opinionated and wish to leave their thumbprint on their work for posterity. It takes special talents to train or to manage the very young. I am referring to those who have no or very little job experience. These workers try to relate how they are to perform with standards learned at school or observed at home.

Some larger companies have introductory courses for young employees. The fast food service employees are usually funneled into a standard uniform and pointed to a spot on the floor and told "This is your space." There are probably more people who get their start at some form of food service than any other business. I would also venture a guess that there are more young people working in the food service industry than any other. While serving hamburgers may not be a person's ultimate goal, it is a good training ground, teaching sound business logic, and more importantly, teaching how to manage money and work as part of a group. Learning teamwork on the ball field is important, but on the ball field or on the court, there is usually a superstar for the rookies to emulate. In the work place you are an employee number. It is a humbling experience. Learning to wash dishes for the first time at work can put you in your place so to speak.

I once had a young rich girl work for me as a wait-ress. It was her first job and she wasn't used to work-ing with others. She told me at home her mother paid other people to do things. After several months she fi-nally began to fit in and her finely colored manicured nails began to chip. Her mother came in one evening with the family for dinner and told me, "You know our daughter has actually started to help around the house without being told, we are really surprised with her progress." This is the same girl who only a few months before was considered a snob by many, and was now a very popular employee.

Older employees can be just as enthusiastic as their younger counterparts. I had a waitress that I called "Bruce" because I could never remember her name. I never did have a good memory for names. Not being able to recall the names of your employees is poor man-agement. Finally one day while at a civic function she introduced me to her boy friend. I thanked her by using her wrong name and I said, "I am just going to call you 'Bruce' because I can remember that." Soon everyone in the restaurant was calling her 'Bruce', and even our regular customer did. She knew everyone in our small town by first name and knew most of their children and some of their pets. She was a real asset. Bruce did have a bad habit of 'visiting' tables during busy times. She would see someone she hadn't seen in a long time and would stop and catch up on gossip. On one very busy Friday night she had wandered up front around the corner with a fresh pot of coffee to serve some of her customers, and ended up in a long-winded gossip conversation. After about ten minutes, not wanting to embarrass her in front of her customers, but wishing to prod her into returning to her other duties, I sent the bus boy up front to tell her that I said the coffee was getting cold. I waited for a few minutes and the bus boy came back with the coffee pot, he said "Bruce told me to give this to you, and that you would know what to do with it."

Most employees carry with them some good skills. Unfortunately most of these same workers have off-setting shortcomings, too. It is up to management to separate these virtues and to accentuate the positive during the working hours. This cannot be accomplished if the employee is a number on a work schedule. There must be an immediate supervisor in charge of any group of workers, and it is their responsibility to observe talented individuals and pass the information along to the people who can better analyze and formulate their talents to the fullest. A talented employee working beneath their potential will be unhappy. Their own personal productivity will suffer as well as their self respect.

Channeling youthful exuberance into personal productivity can be testing for any manager because of their talents and desire to charge ahead. Getting it done right doesn't seem to be as important as getting it done. There is the time old saying, "If you have time to do it over then you have time to do it right the first time." The manager with the talents to direct a group such as this must have flexibility and patience, along with the much needed wisdom that must always be available, if not present. Because of their energetic nature, youth must be molded to perform the duties for which they were hired. The inflexible manager will not be able to bend with the constant challenges and questions he will encounter with the youth.

Military leadership can be far more rigid because that is how the military system is designed. Follow the leader is the topic for the day's duty roster and to disobey a leader is cause for disciplinary action. In the public sector this will not work. An employee would change jobs rather than to be subject to this type of leadership.

I have found in many cases, if an employer can hire a good freshman or sophomore high school student and put him in a job that is challenging and one that he can grow with, the student will most likely be with you all through high school. Having a good base of high school students is a valuable asset when it comes time to train new students. The old ones with job knowledge and with a good regard for the system can easily help to train the new recruits. Remember, when you pair up the old with the new, match personalities as well as possible. I sometimes enjoy listening to the older employee berate the new ones. They do not need to be as tactful as management and are not liable to harassment charges. Peer pressure can sometimes do more to change a situation than good management.

Reward excellence, acknowledge poor performance, but do not dwell on it. Always offer a better way; give your employees a way out. Employees, even the lesser qualified ones do not want to be associated with failure, so keep the jobs matched to their abilities, give them help and incentives. Don't be the kind of boss who reminds them of their parents when they go home by telling them, "You will never amount to anything." Be sensitive to personality change and, unfortunately during these times, be on guard for drug or alcohol use. Drugs in the work place are prevalent. Offer drug and alcohol treatment programs for your workers. Call your local health clinics and arrange for treatment for those employees who request it. Above all keep a strict code of silence for those with problems. Never fire a drug or alcohol user because of their addiction. Suspend them if all else fails until they accept the treatment offered by the company. Let your work force know that you are trying to work with them and will not use their dependency as a reason to terminate them.

chapter 11

THE 'WAY' OF the manager is to tell the plain and simple truth. Managing is not a contest of eloquence. It is far more important to act in behalf of the whole group than it is to win individual arguments. Your work force is not a debating team. It is far more important to react wisely to what is happening than it is to be able to explain everything in terms of management theories. Your work force is not grading your decisions. The 'way' of the manager is not to showcase a string of successes. The wise leader is busy helping others find their own personal successes. Sharing success with others breeds success, and so it goes. The 'way' of the manager is to find reward in personal satisfaction like the kind that comes with helping someone else reach their goal.

While dealing with the employees you may at times find yourself engaged in an argument, and if the outcome is not in your favor, then you must compromise for the benefit of the "cause." Be gracious while yielding your position. It is not the 'way' of the manager in business to be right or to win arguments, nor is it your duty to find flaws in the other person's position, nor is it the 'way' of the manager to feel impugned if he loses an argument. It is the 'way' of the manager to facilitate whatever is happening for the good of the company. If we are all working for the same cause as one body, there is no side to take. Remember, it is the accomplishment of the common goal that must outweigh all personal prejudices. Once the goal is achieved then all can take part in the glory. It is important to remember that the group will not profit if the leader tries to take the credit for all the work that has been done. Any leader who feels he must control his employees with strict policies in order to make things come out his way, will find that the co-worker will resist against his wishes. When a leader can only be critical without being positive, he will find that he has taken the life and enthusiasm out of his workers and their personal productivity as well. The 'way' of the manager is not to be greedy, defensive, or selfish. The 'way' of the manager is to lead by creating the need and allowing the workers to reach their own personal level of greatness and help achieve a common goal. If a manager has a work force, it is apparent that he cannot complete the task without help. So he must maintain a smooth relationship with those he manages and keep the lines of communication open. The employees must feel the manager's enthusiasm and his importance to complete each task so it may be done on time and without error.

The manager's glory comes in being able to lead his workers together in the accomplishment of the team goal, and it is the glory of the team for having the skills to get him there. There is an old saying, "Catch your employees doing something right." We expect our employees to do their jobs correctly, which is why we hired them. We do not expect them to make mistakes and when they do, we acknowledge them with verbal or written notice. When we walk through the work place inspecting the various facets of the job, it is a necessary step for management to stop by each worker when possible and make a positive remark like, "Nice work." or something similar. Positive reinforcement is a valuable tool and unfortunately, it is one of the least used tool in our tool box. The tools that seem to get most of the work are the wrecking tools—tools that tear down, undercut, belittle, or find fault with those whom we are working with. Tearing down doesn't take any particular skill or talent however, building requires procedures to be followed, in proper order, and with good forethought. Building up the character of the work force responds in the same manner.

Most people are familiar with their own faults or shortcomings. They do not need management to point them out. After all, they have most likely had those most of their lives. "Positive reinforcement", or picking out the areas where the co-workers show improvement, or even a developed skill, is where the main emphasis should be placed. Telling a brick layer that his rows of bricks is the most evenly spaced and his angles are the most accurate you've seen is positive reinforcement. In the same vein telling him that if he could just pick up a little speed he might well be the best brick layer in the company will challenge him. We have just inserted a negative in a positive way so as to challenge the integrity of the employee to be better. Isn't it better than coming up to this same employee on the job and telling him that all the other brick layers in his section have been done for a long time and asking him why is he so slow?

A short-order cook in a restaurant has ten recooks one night and the manager berates him telling him how much money he is throwing away, and asks "What is the matter with you, anyway?" First of all the cook will probably just hide his mistakes to keep the manager off his case and not try to improve. The manager should approach the cook by saying "I notice you had one less recook than the night before, and I appreciate your helping to control food cost." Then the manager tells him if he can have an entire shift without a recook, he will buy him dinner. Don't you suppose the cook will have a better attitude and make a more honest effort to try and reach the goal set forth by his manager?

There is almost always a positive way to deliver a negative type of statement. This is usually done by extolling the virtues of the person first, and then following it up by saying, "If we could only improve in this one area, we would be almost perfect." Reinforce the positive and then follow up by stating your purpose in a softer tone. This keeps you from sounding like you are demanding perfection from your workers. It is a sad time when an employee comes up to you and says, "Don't you ever have anything nice to say?" Your first impulse would be to say, "Of course I do." Then you would probably stop and try to think of something to say without looking foolish. Remember that the 'way' of management, the 'way' of strategy, is how things happen. However, how things happen is not the same as what you should do when things happen.

Your freedom of choice is your responsibility to make the right decision; no one can make it for you. Instead of seeking advice you must learn to be more conscious of what is actually happening around you. You must learn to retreat to the center so you may better see the whole. Then you will be able to see how things happen and make your decisions as to what to do. Again it is not the 'way' to preach or dictate behavior. Each person is responsible for his own behavior and a responsible person will follow all natural laws. These laws are the laws of God and of man. These laws are so general that they cover all possible events and so specific that they apply to every instance of any event. It is up to you to decide what to do in any given situation.

Managing is exciting, rewarding, and most of all challenging. But while there is much to benefit, the manager for all his efforts like personal satisfaction, advancement, and better pay, there is a very serious side to management that must be considered—all decisions where employees are a part of the answer. A manager who controls the work force of his company is also directly involved in the personal lives of each person under his control. The livelihood and general well being of the families related to his co-workers depend on how he treats them. Giving out raises or giving out overtime hours, or even cutting back certain projects directly relates to the income for the families of the co-workers in question. Taking food from their mouths may not be something you want to take into consideration when you make decisions regarding pay, bonuses, etc. None the less the awesome burden is still there. Do not let me lead you to misunderstand your responsibility to the 'way'. We cannot simply look at our workers and decide who needs money the most and then give these people the best shifts. We need to give our best and most productive workers the best shifts. The loyal individuals who have stuck it out during times of near crisis should be given special consideration for having hung in there. If you have two 'like' employees for instance doing the same job and for whatever reason one of the jobs should be eliminated, it is then a matter of which employee should be let go. If one of the two people is a student living at home and the other person is a family member working to pay household bills, then this should be considered, even if the student is a better worker. Hopefully, there can be a compromise where the hours can be divided so that each may earn enough to sustain them until a transfer or job retraining can bring one of them to a new position. Remember the famous Christmas Classic, "A Christmas Carol," where Scrooge fired Tiny Tim's father on Christmas Eve? This kind of thing happens frequently in the real world of business. If you must take a person's livelihood away from them, at least leave them with their dignity and self-respect. It is one thing to terminate someone, it is another to humiliate them in the process.

Confucius Said ...

There is no correct way to suspend, terminate, or lay someone off work. There is usually a humane way, try to find it.

chapter 12

DURING THE YEARS I have spent writing this book, I would find myself practicing with earnest those things I was writing about at the same time with a more dedicated interest. I suppose I was something like the intern studying disease symptoms who would have the symptom of each disease by the time the class was over. It was during this time an incident happened to me while I was managing a shift in my restaurant that upset me completely. It was a busy weekend night and the dishes were coming out of the dish room slower than usual. There are not many things more embarrassing than not to have clean silverware to serve the customers with. After the third trip to the dish room to encourage my two young teenage boys to hurry up, trying to explain to them the urgency of the situation, I found them washing steak plates, (steak plates are easier to wash and do not require sorting), unlike the silverware. Well my frustration got the best of me. I was challenged by two dishwashers. I lost my cool for just a few seconds and yelled my disgust, then I left the area.

For the rest of the evening I was upset that I let the two young dishwashers get the best of me. I felt that I had failed to use all the tools that I know how to use and that I should go back and rewrite that particular chapter. I discussed this event with several close friends, and they helped me through it reminding me that the person in my book was real as far as the perfect role model was; however, in real life and during all the various circumstances there was never an absolute, as far as making the best management decision was concerned. This brings me to an all important point. If a person was to read all the management books ever written and by some quirk of nature was able to memorize them, he would still not be the perfect manager. There will never be a book written that could handle or explain all the various problems management can expect to find in real life. If such a book could be written, there isn't a library large enough to hold all the volumes. Therefore, it is natural to make mistakes while dealing with employees, and although mistakes are never well received, knowing that we made them gives us food for thought. It's the sensitive manager that is aware of his error and will rethink the situation, putting the incident in his memory bank for the next time a similar situation develops. I have found it necessary from time to time to go to an employee and apologize for having accused them for some action that they didn't cause. I have also found that being able to apologize for an incident, that was more my mistake than someone else's, brought me more respect from the work force. That is to say, for the occasional mistake, not ones that occur regularly.

Confucius Said ...

A young paper boy who delivered my afternoon paper every evening would stop in my restaurant and I would give him a free soda. Sometimes we would chat about local events. He lived across the street and was a fine polite young man. One day when he came in for his drink and to deliver the paper he greeted me with his usual cheerful smile and a hello. I was having a remarkably bad day and I was short with him. Although I do not remember what it was I said, I do remember his reply, and I shall for the rest of my life.

"When someone is having a bad day isn't it remarkable how they always seem to find a way to let others know about it."

I just looked at this young man and thought about the old saying, "Out of the mouths of babes…"

I remember just looking at him for several seconds thinking about what he had just said and pondered the wisdom. We all have bad days as well as good ones. It seems like we would rather make sure more people know when we are in a bad mood than hen we are in a good one.

I was attending a leadership conference many years ago when one of our guest speakers, whose name fails me, said "Big people share ideas, small people have secrets." And on it goes. Successful people don't feel challenged because they are confident in their ability while small-minded people pretend that their successes are due to some magic formula and they are not about to pass it on.

The premise on which this book was written is "There are no new ideas, only very old ones that keep getting updated so they sound current." While the ideas are not new, the way we explain them is. After we hear them, usually, we can relate to the same words only said in a different manner. This reinforces the ideas and gives them more meaning. It's like old jokes that keep coming back with different characters but the punch lines are always the same. When something works really well we tend to keep it around. We constantly learn and then relearn ideas and concepts that are more important to us until they become second nature. While this book on management principles is the closest thing to the 'way' of management for many years, it must be remembered that the concept goes back thousands of years. Hopefully, those who read this book will find much useful food for thought and be able to project some of the concepts into their daily management activity. Maybe some of these stories will remind you of other stories you have heard before and reinforce their message. It should be remembered, while it seems like there are no new ideas, only old ones reborn, thousands of years ago there was no such thing as technology, drug abuse, or modern medicine. Therefore we must also remember that while the basic concepts of management are the same their application in many areas of today's work place are being reinvented continuously.

We can deal with these new advanced concepts by beginning with the age old basics. Once the basics are understood then they can be tailored to properly fit in new positions. Like the advanced math that goes into the technology for sending spaceships to the moon. The math still uses basic addition and subtraction to make the formulas work. We need to remember here, or at least it should be noted here, that managing people is basic and standard in many aspects. Managing alcoholics or drug abusers takes talent of a different nature. The old adage, "You can't talk sense to a drunk." also holds true for those on drugs. People who are in altered states of consciousness because of a chemical dependency can only be trusted to do one thing, deceive. These people begin with deceiving themselves first and then others because they have lost their true perspective of reality. People with dependency problems may or may not be talented. They are not dependable and they must be given the same set of rules to follow the rest of the work force has.

I have used people with drug problems many times with the agreement they would seek medical or professional help. I would help offset the cost as long as they would follow the program. Drug and alcohol abusers are still people and can be brought into the working mainstream with proper care. Remember the care in handling people with dependencies is far more intense than normal, so be prepared to spend extra time and energy.

Another group of workers that must be addressed are those with handicaps, physical and/or mental. I worked with the handicapped on a regular basis. They are usually slower, but far more intense and are more likely to be on time and have fewer sick days than their 'normal' counterparts. The community respects the employer who hires the physically and mentally handicapped. The rules and regulations are still the same. There must be some consideration to physical handicaps to facilitate movement. I have found them to be cheerful and generally enthusiastic. Sometimes working with them for a few minutes has helped me to overcome some temporary down times.

It has been said that a manager is like a coach. The coach leads the team to a common goal, and is responsible for the game plan to get them there. It has also been said the coach deserves the team he has. I suppose that is why in professional sports, whenever a team is having a losing season, it is usually the coach who is replaced first. The coach scouts around for the right person to fill the position on the team. Like the manager looks to hire right the employee to fill a vacancy. The team reflects the attitude of the coach and the better the coach, the better the attitude of the team. Of course a sports coach can demand the team follow his game plan to the letter or else. The manager must seek out the same type of results by managing. Follow the 'way' and you will not get lost.

In closing

THERE WAS A day in my life when God chose to teach me one of life's important lessons. I was staying at a beach-front hotel while attending a business conference. It rained the entire time of the conference. One evening just before sunset the rain abated and the sun struggled to break through its cloud-like cage. I took the opportunity to walk along the low-tide exposed beach in search of washed up treasures, and enjoyed the smells only a beach can have. I was attracted to the many types and colors of seashells. Like a small child, I began picking up all the shells I could hold until I could hold no more. I made a decision to save only the whole shells and not the broken ones. It was quickly apparent that only the very small shells were whole and undamaged. I found no large shells unchipped or unbroken. I sat on a sand dune with my hand filled with shells and pondered the situation. It was then I realized the shells were reflecting the roles we all play in life. The shells were damaged to varying degrees as a result of rolling around the ocean floor during storms, bouncing off rocks and being abused by other sea creatures. The seashells helped me to understand the human life cycle. Man cannot go through life without bumps bruises and scars, unless of course he spends his whole life locked in a closet.

ABOUT THE AUTHOR

W.J. "DUKE" MADER has helped hire and train several thousand employees. He has been retained by national companies to help improve their bottom line. He has held seminars and training classes for numerous companies and has written sales training manuals. He is a member of Mensa and a Board Certified Forensic Examiner. He has achieved the "Humanitarian Service Award" from United Cerebral Palsy. W.J. "Duke" Mader has found the best 'way' to accomplish a task is to follow the 'way' of the manager.

You are invited to visit his photography website:
www.photographybyduke.com